Coloring Note

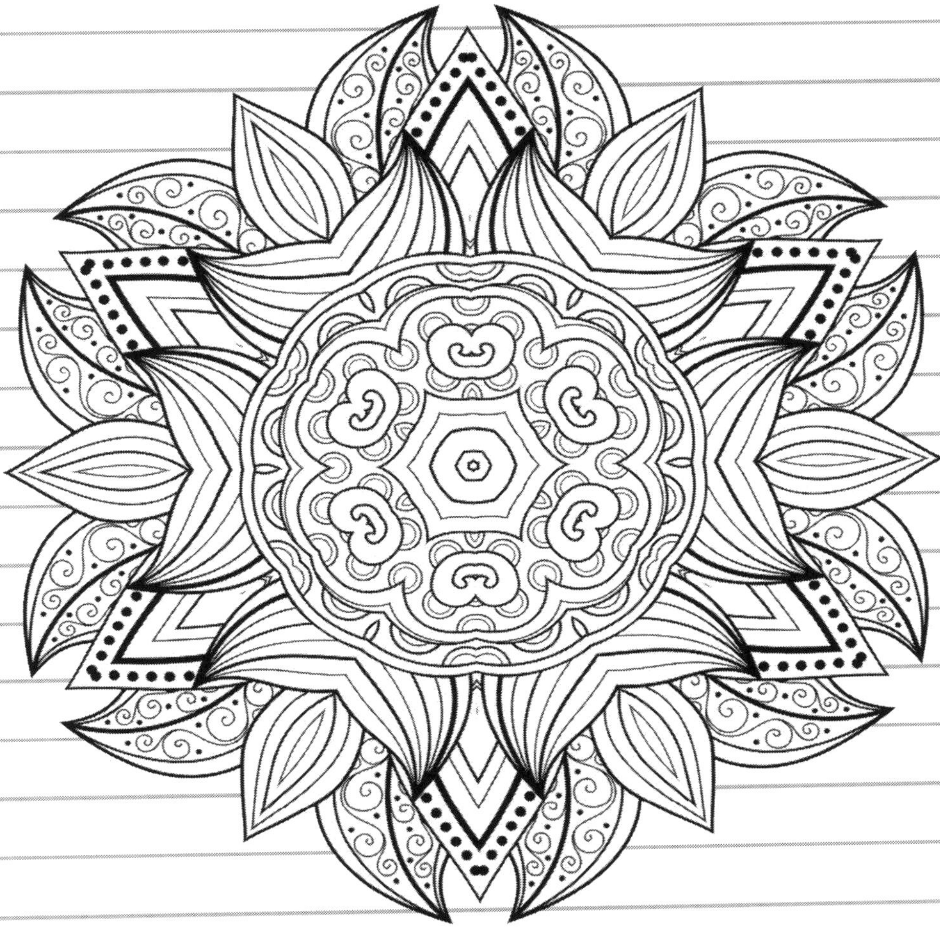

ZenMaster Coloring Books

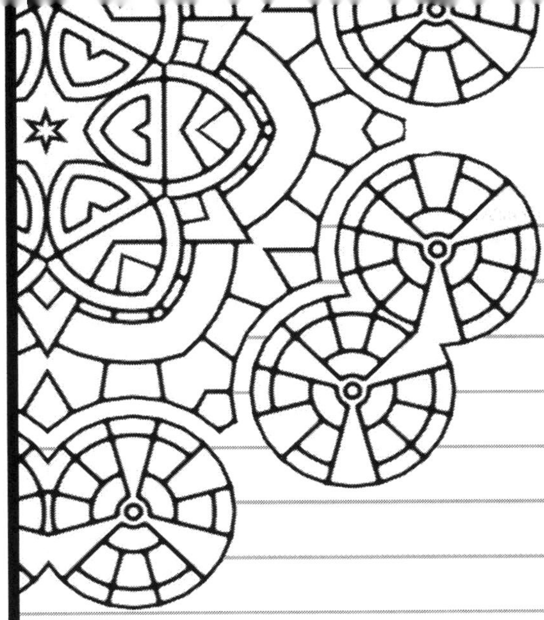

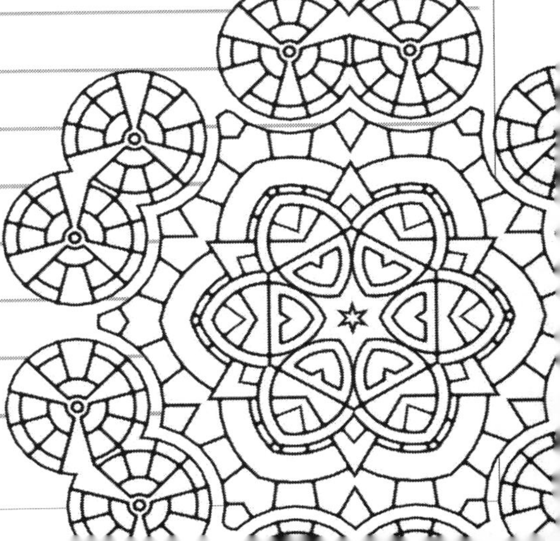

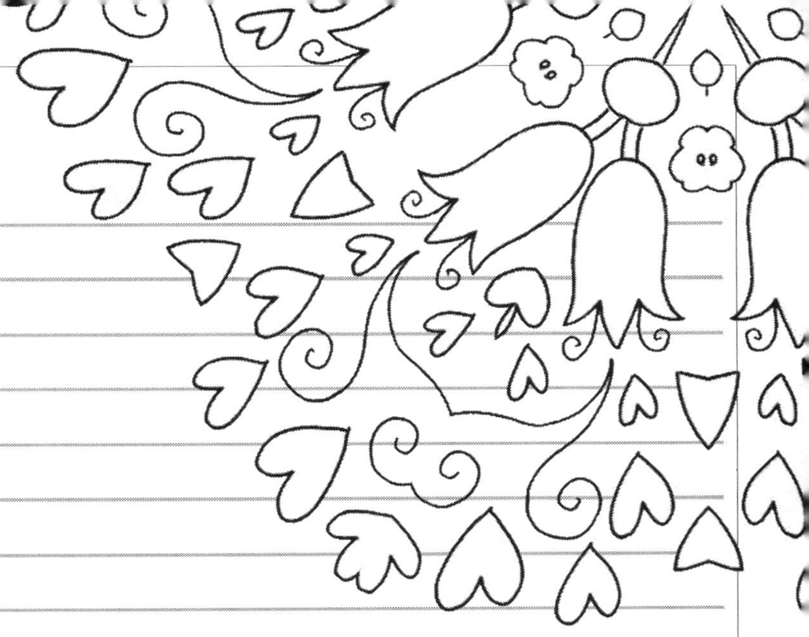

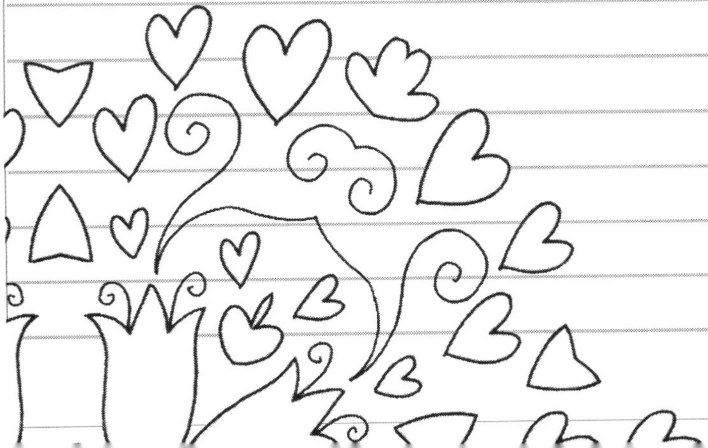

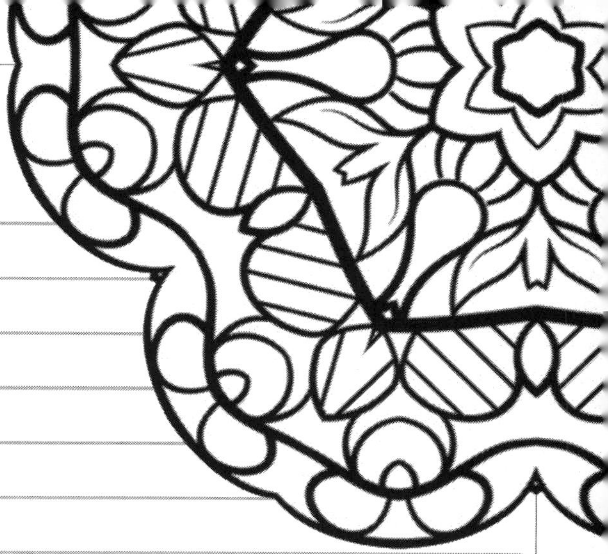

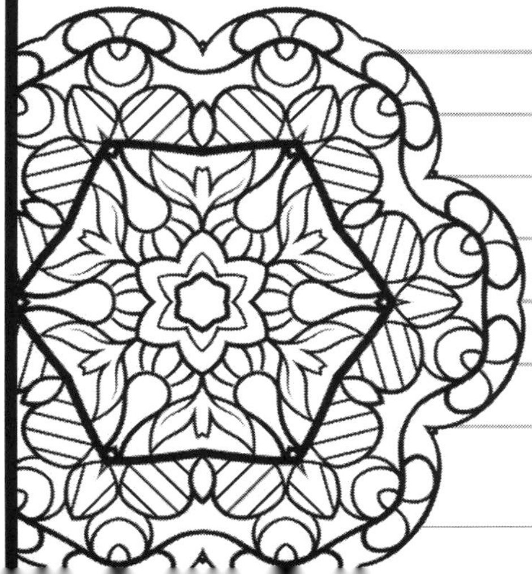

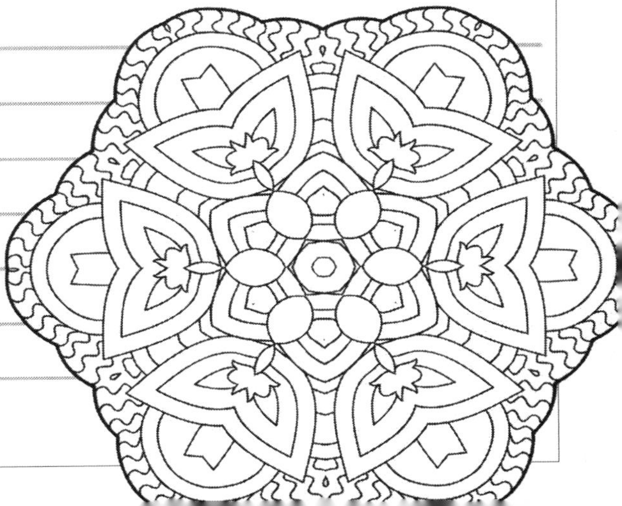

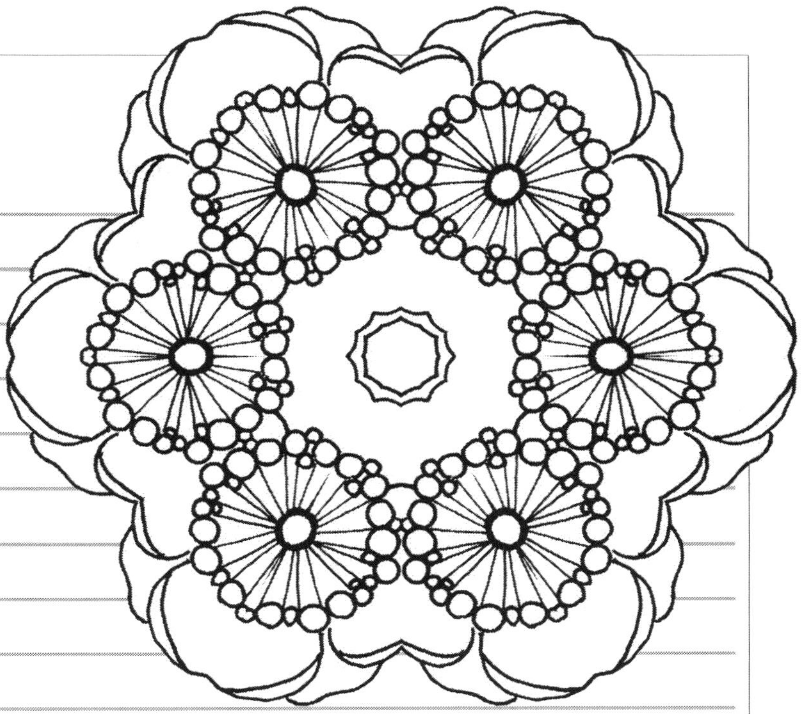

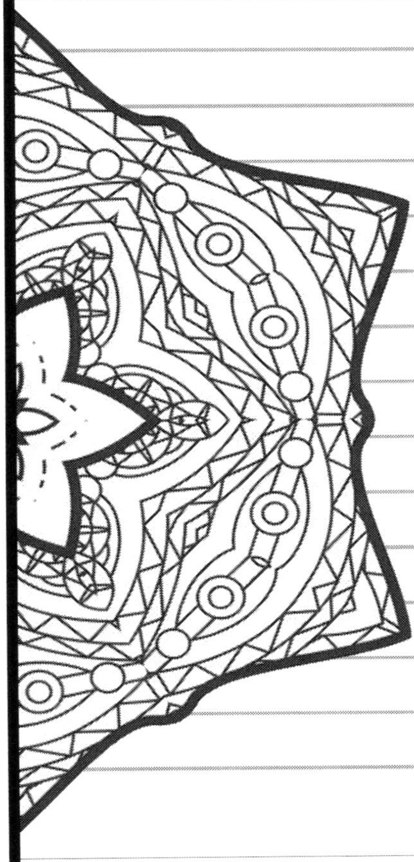

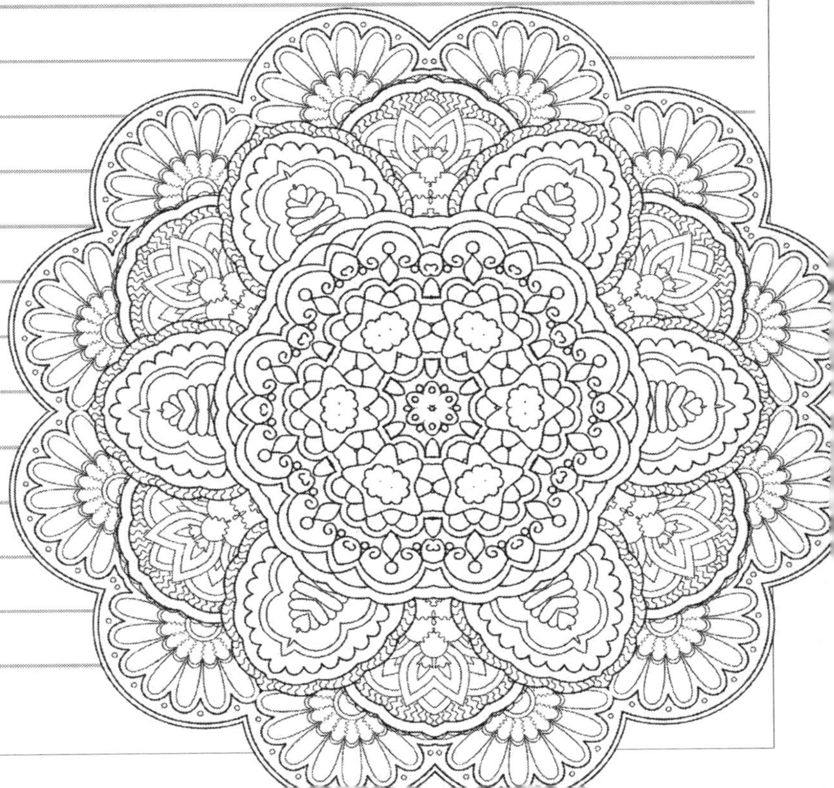

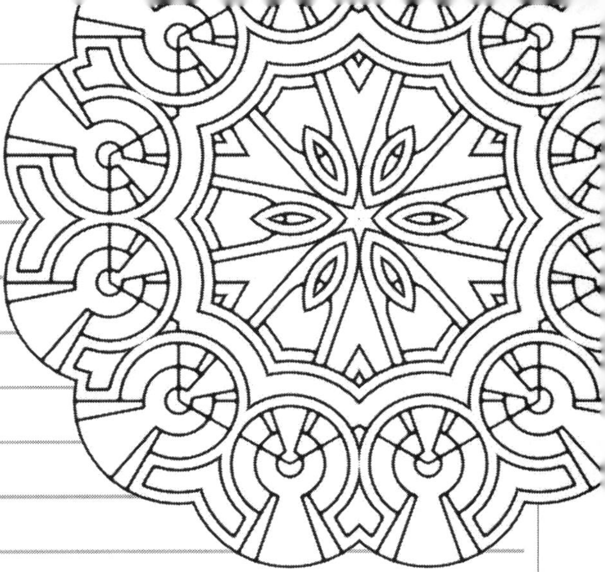

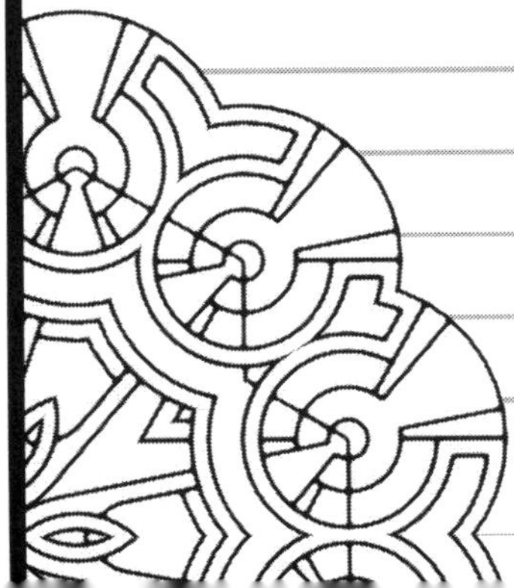

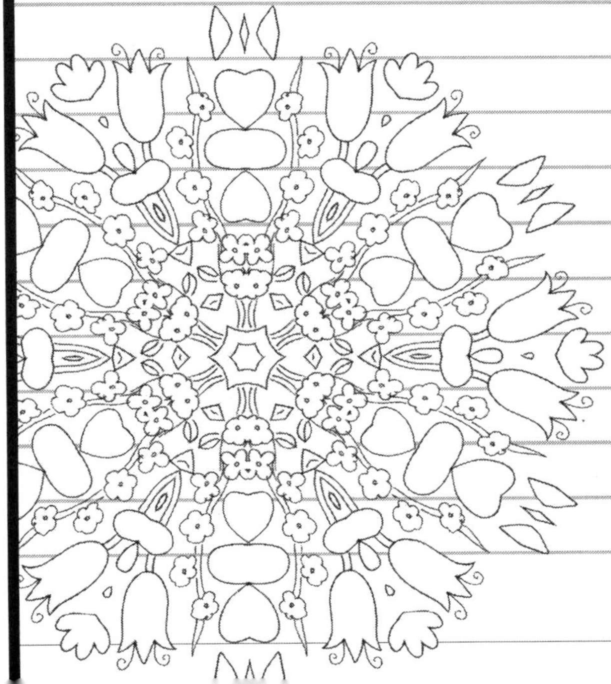

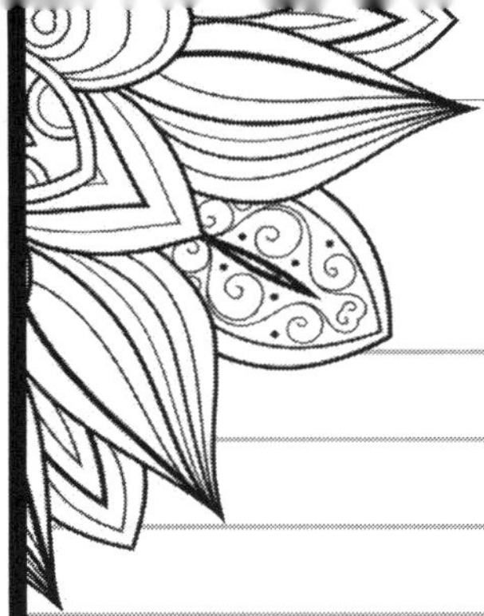

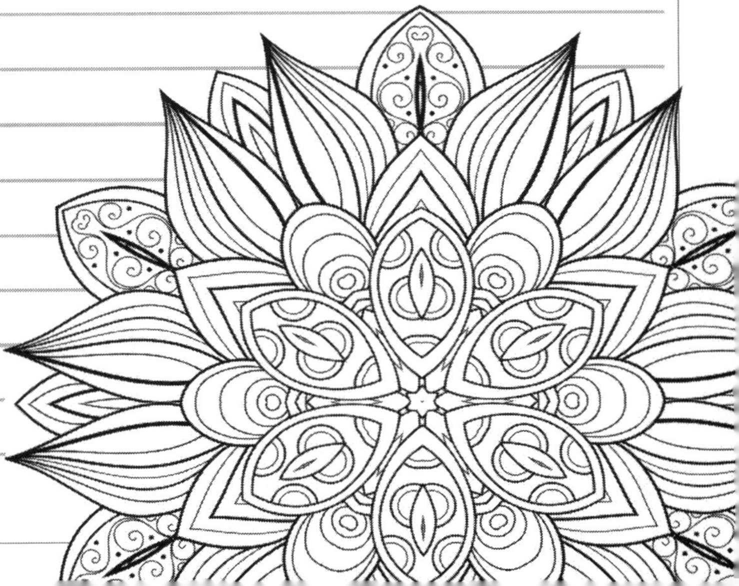

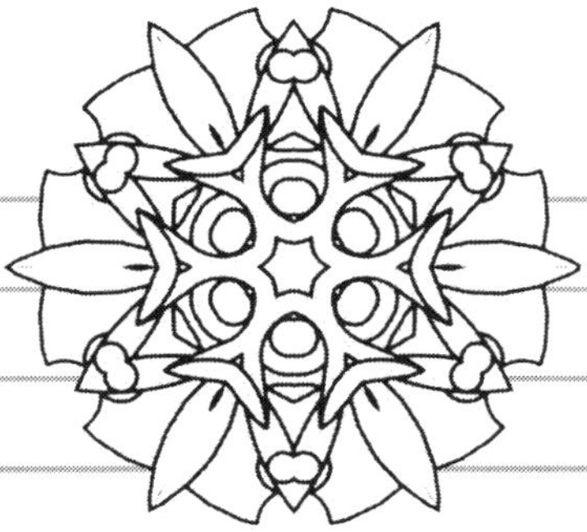

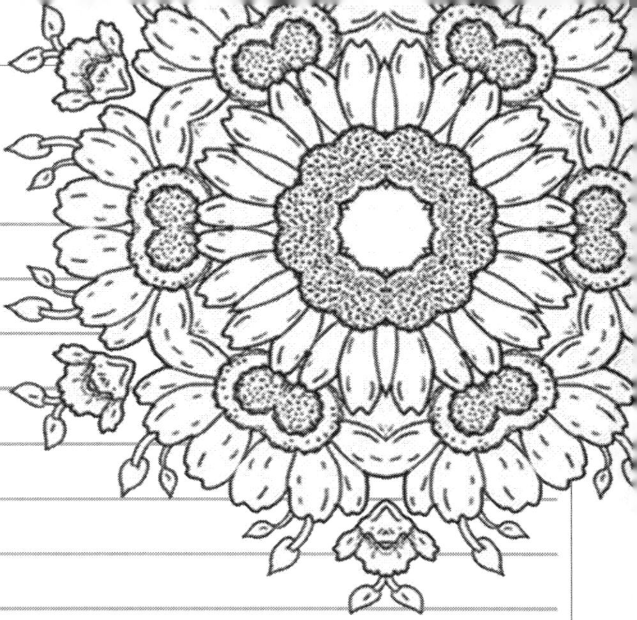

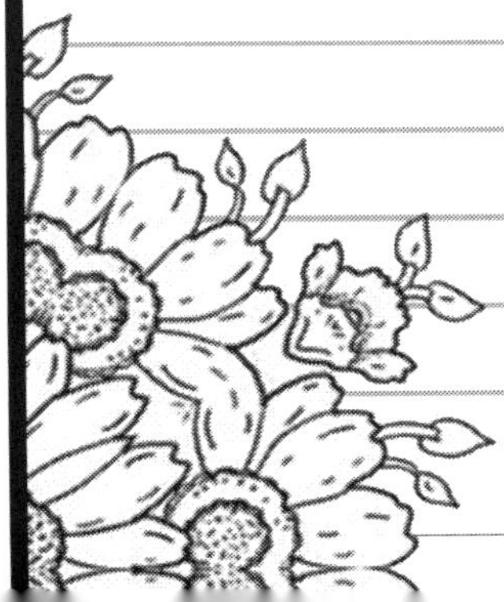

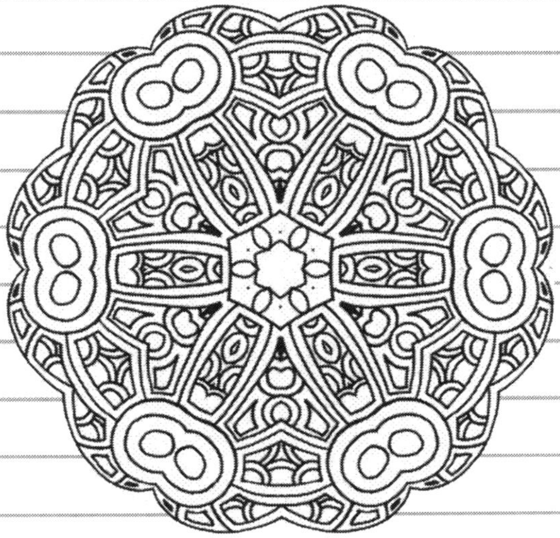

Made in the USA
Middletown, DE
12 July 2025

10481451R00057